Andrea Palladio

Andrea Palladio

teNeues

Editor in chief:
Paco Asensio

Archipockets coordination:
Aurora Cuito

Editor and original texts:
Llorenç Bonet

Photographs:
© Pino Guidolotti (p.guidolotti@libero.it)

English translation:
Mathew Clark

German translation:
Bettina Beck

French translation:
Michel Ficerai

Italian translation:
Giovanna Carnevali

Graphic design / Layout:
Emma Termes Parera and Soti Mas-Bagà

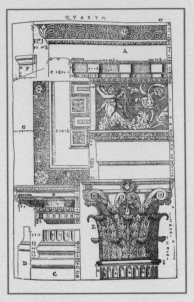

Published worldwide by teNeues Publishing Group
(except Spain, Portugal and South-America):

teNeues Book Division
Neuer Zollhof 1, 40221 Düsseldorf, Germany
Tel: 0049-(0)211-994597-0
Fax: 0049-(0)211-994597-40

teNeues Publishing Company
16 West 22nd Street, New York, N.Y., 10010, USA
Tel.: 001-212-627-9090
Fax: 001-212-627-9511

teNeues Publishing UK Ltd.
Aldwych House, 71/91 Aldwych
London WC2B 4HN, UK
Tel.: 0044-1892-837-171
Fax: 0044-1892-837-272

teNeues France S.A.R.L.
140, rue de la Croix Nivert
75015 Paris, France
Tel.: 0033-1-5576-6205
Fax: 0033-1-5576-6419

www.teneues.com

Editorial project:

© 2002 LOFT Publications
Domènech 7-9, 2o 2ª
08012 Barcelona, Spain
Tel.: 0034 932 183 099
Fax: 0034 932 370 060
e-mail: loft@loftpublications.com
www.loftpublications.com

Printed by:
Gráficas Anman. Sabadell, Spain.

September 2002

Die Deutsche Bibliothek – CIP-Einheitsaufnahme
Ein Titeldatensatz für diese Publikation ist bei der Deutschen Bibliothek erhältlich.

ISBN: 3-8238-5541-7

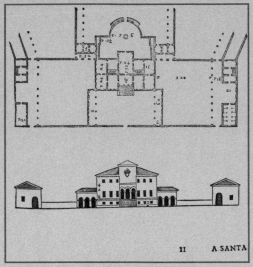

Cover of "I quattro libri dell'
architettura" (1570), by Andrea Palladio

Plan and elevation of Villa Godi

"La città non sia altro che una casa grande, e per lo contrario la casa, una città picola"

A. Palladio. Libro II, capítulo 12
Venice, 1570

In the mid-seventeenth century the once all-powerful Venetian merchants became aware that their little republic couldn't compete with the great European empires. These cosmopolitan nobles were forced to transform their businesses due to the crisis in the Mediterranean brought on by the upsurge in trans-Atlantic trading. This new situation led them to invest their fortunes on dry land: they turned the region's marshes into soil fit for agriculture and they moved from the cities to the country to oversee their farms in person, although they did not renounce their noble past and their city ways. All this called for buildings that not only served for exploiting the land but also indicated that their owners were not mere country folk but city nobles. Moreover, the financial precariousness of this transition required buildings that could be put up in stages, in keeping with their owners' cashflow.

This is the context that witnessed the emergence of Andrea di Pietro della Gondola, called Palladio by his mentor, Giangiorgio Trissino. It was this humanist, the most outstanding intellectual in Vicenza – one of the cities that paid tribute to Venice – who discovered the stonemason Andrea di Pietro, then aged thirty, and gave him a classical education on seeing his willingness to learn and propensity for mathematics.

Palladio was trained as a technician with a solid basis in humanist learning rather than as a humanist in the strictest terms. He knew the works of Vitruvius and Alberti, but he was a practising architect and not a theoretician, as can be seen from his "Quattro Libri" (Venice, 1570), where he focuses more on pragmatic architectural solutions than on theoretical questions.

Palladio proved to be surprisingly versatile. All his villas belong to the same architectural family; their starting point was a main unit in the form of a square, with no central courtyard but usually adorned with the typical "brachese" (porticos for farming tools) on the sides, but the end result was always adapted to the particular needs of the owner. This distinctive trait has been constantly stressed by modern commentators; it was as if Palladio had a very clear mental picture of the characteristics of this type of building and adapted this idealized villa to the budget, the setting and the functions that it had to serve. However, the underlying concept was not idealism but the use of modules: Palladio's repertory may have been limited but he could combine the various pieces at his disposal in any number of ways. Perhaps the clearest examples in this respect are the main entrances: these are always based on classical ped-

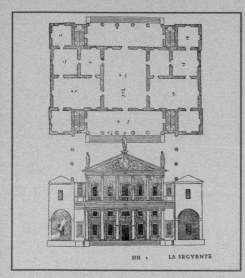

Plan and elevation of Villa Valmanara

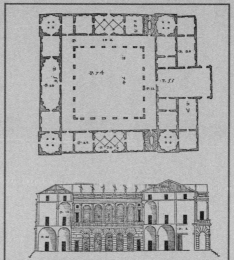

Plan and elevation of Palacio Thiene

iments but, although they may be similar and have features in common, no two are identical and there is always evidence of new developments.

Palladio's buildings are not merely practical; they have an undeniable beauty, often derived from the simplicity of their elements and a certain sense of restraint. These characteristics are particularly apparent in the work from his Venetian period and his religious projects: San Giorgio Maggiore and Il Redentore.

Palladio won success as an architect who understood the noblemen of Vicenza, those former merchants who had gone on to set themselves up as landowners, and he built them practical, comfortable and salubrious houses with inexpensive materials. This mentality is similar to that of the cottage culture of English noblemen, as well as that of the great American landowners, who were highly pragmatic but also loved the monumentality and classical echoes of Palladian architecture. The distinguishing features of these Anglo-Saxon societies, combined with the success of Palladio's "Quattro Libri" and the fact that Venice became a reference point for England in the eighteenth century, explain the great historical impact of Palladio's works, making him the most copied architect of all time.

In der Mitte des 16. Jahrhunderts sind sich die vormals mächtigen venezianischen Kaufleute darüber bewusst, dass es ihre kleine Republik nicht mit den europäischen Großreichen aufnehmen kann. Sie sind eine adlige, kosmopolitische Klasse, die ihre Geschäfte aufgrund der Krise, unter der das Mittelmeer angesichts der Macht des Atlantikhandels leidet, umstellen muss. Diese neue Situation führt dazu, dass sie ihr Vermögen in der Terraferma (festes Land) anlegen. Die sumpfigen Gebiete der Region verwandeln sie in urbares Land und begeben sich von den Städten dorthin, um die Betriebe persönlich zu leiten. So ist für die landwirtschaftlichen Gutshöfe eine funktionelle Architektur gefragt, die aber zugleich berücksichtigt, dass die Besitzer eben nicht nur Bauern, sondern adlige Städter sind. Zudem erfordert es das wirtschaftliche Risiko dieses Übergangsstadiums, dass die Gebäude je nach Liquidität des Eigentümers nach und nach gebaut werden können.

In diesem Zusammenhang erscheint Andrea di Pietro della Gondola, von seinem Mentor, Giangiorgio Trissino, Palladio genannt. Trissino ist einer der prominentesten Intellektuellen von Vicenza, einer der Städte, die an Venedig Tribut zahlt. Der Humanist entdeckt den damals 30-jährigen Stein-

Villa Almerico, la Rotonda

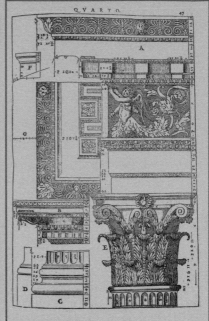

Corinthian order, published in the book "I quattro libri dell'architettura" (1570), by Andrea Palladio

metz Andrea di Pietro und ermöglicht ihm eine klassische
Ausbildung, nachdem er auf dessen Lernbereitschaft und
seine Neigung zur Mathematik aufmerksam geworden war.
Er kennt zwar die Texte Vitruvs und Albertis, ist aber selbst
eher ein praktischer als ein theoretischer Baumeister. Dies
zeigt sich in seinen „Quattro Libri" (Die vier Bücher der
Architektur, Venedig, 1570), in denen er sich mehr für die
pragmatischen Lösungen als für die theoretischen Proble-
me der Architektur interessiert.
Palladio legt eine erstaunliche Vielseitigkeit an den Tag.
Alle seine Villen gehören der gleichen architektonischen
Familie an. Den Ausgangspunkt bildet ein quadratischer
Hauptkörper ohne Innenhof, der an den Seiten nahezu
immer über die typischen „brachese" (Säulenvorbauten zur
Verwahrung der landwirtschaftlichen Geräte) verfügt. Die
Villen sind jedoch stets den Bedürfnissen des jeweiligen
Besitzers angepasst. Sämtliche Studien des 20. Jahrhunderts heben diese einzigartige Facette des Baumeisters
aus Vicenza hervor. Offenbar hat Palladio eine sehr klare
Vorstellung von den Anforderungen an diese Gebäude, die
es ihm ermöglicht, die gedachte Villa an den bestehenden
finanziellen Rahmen, das Gelände und die von ihr zu erfül-
lenden Funktionen anzupassen. Er geht bei seinen Kon-
struktionen von einem begrenzten Repertoire verschiede-
ner Module aus, was eine unendliche Anzahl von
Kombinationen zulässt. Vielleicht sind in dieser Hinsicht die

Haupteingänge das deutlichste Element. Alle entspringen
der Vorstellung des klassischen Säulenvorbaus und weisen
teilweise ähnliche oder gemeinsame Lösungen auf. Es gibt
jedoch keine Wiederholungen, da stets eine Entwicklung zu
erkennen ist.
Die Gebäude Palladios sind praktisch und darüber hinaus
von unbestreitbarer Schönheit, die in vielen Fällen auf der
Einfachheit ihrer Bestandteile und einem gewissen Begriff
von Nüchternheit beruht. Diese Eigenschaften kommen am
stärksten in den Sakralbauten aus Palladios venezianischer
Zeit, San Giorgio Maggiore und Il Redentore, zum Ausdruck.
Er tut sich als derjenige Baumeister hervor, der den Adel
von Vicenza versteht, dessen Vertreter sich von Kaufleuten
zu Landbesitzern entwickelten. Diese Geisteshaltung
ähnelt der der englischen Adligen mit ihrer Cottage-Kultur
und auch jener der großen nordamerikanischen Landbesit-
zer, die pragmatisch orientiert und gleichzeitig Liebhaber
der palladianischen Monumentalbauten und ihres klassischen Erscheinungsbildes sind. Die Eigenschaften der
angelsächsischen Gesellschaft im Zusammenspiel mit
dem Erfolg der „Quattro Libri" Palladios und der Tatsache,
dass Venedig ab dem 18. Jahrhundert eine Bezugsgröße
für England war, erklären das enorme historische Vermögen der Werke Palladios, des am meisten nachgeahmten
Baumeisters der Geschichte.

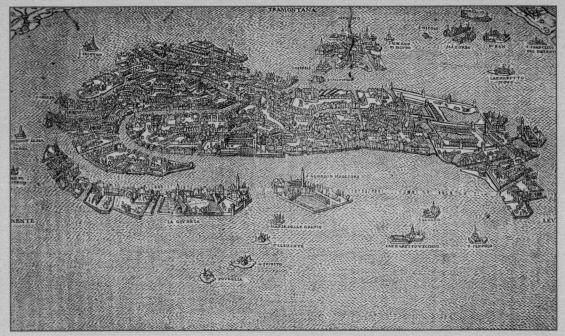

View of Venice, published in the book "Vitrvvii Pollionis de architectura" (1567), edition by Daniel Barbaro

Au milieu du XVIème siècle, les commerçants vénitiens, autrefois tout puissants, prennent conscience que leur petite république ne peut concurrencer les grands empires européens. Ils appartiennent à une noblesse cosmopolite qui doit reconvertir ses affaires en raison de la crise accablant la Méditerranée, sous la poussée du commerce atlantique. L'investissement de leurs fortunes sur la terre ferme devient un point de passage obligé : ils transforment les terrains marécageux de la région en une terre cultivable et déménagent des villes aux champs afin de diriger personnellement les exploitations, sans oublier la noblesse de leur passé et leurs habitudes urbaines. De là une architecture fonctionnelle pour les exploitations horticoles, tenant compte du fait que les maîtres sont désormais non seulement des paysans mais aussi de nobles citadins. De plus, face à la fragilité économique de cette transition, il s'avère nécessaire que ces constructions puissent être édifiées par étapes, selon la santé financière du propriétaire.

C'est dans ce contexte qu'apparaît Andrea di Pietro della Gondola, nommé Palladio par Giangiorgio Trissino, son mentor et l'intellectuel le plus en vue de Vicenza, une des cités rendant tribut à Venise. C'est précisément cet humaniste qui découvre Andrea di Pietro, alors un tailleur de pierre et sculpteur de trente ans, et qui lui offre une éducation classique, ayant pris la mesure de sa prédispo-

sition à apprendre et de son penchant pour les études mathématiques.

La formation reçue par Andrea est plutôt celle d'un technicien avec des connaissances humanistes plus ou moins étayées, que celle d'un humaniste à proprement parler. Il connaît les textes de Vitruve et d'Alberti, mais c'est un architecte praticien et non théoricien comme il le démontre dans ses « Quattro Libri » (Venise, 1570), où il s'intéresse davantage aux solutions pragmatiques qu'aux problèmes théoriques de l'architecture.

Palladio met en avant une polyvalence étonnante. Toutes ses villas répondent à une même famille architecturale : partant d'un corps principal carré, sans patio central, avec pratiquement systématiquement de typiques « brachese » (portiques pour les outils des champs) latéraux, elles s'adaptent cependant toujours aux impératifs de leur propriétaire spécifique. Toutes les études du XXème siècle relèvent cette facette singulière de l'architecte de Vicenza. Il semble que Palladio ait une image mentale très claire des besoins de ce type de construction et qu'il adapte la villa idéale au budget, au terrain et aux fonctions qui lui sont inhérents. Cependant, il ne fonde pas son travail sur l'idéalisme mais plutôt sur une conception modulaire de l'architecture : il construit en se fondant sur des pièces distinctes, avec un répertoire limité mais selon une combinatoire infinie. Sans doute les éléments les plus

La Basilica

Il Redentore

clairs en ce sens sont-ils les accès principaux : ils trouvent tous leur origine dans l'idée d'un fronton classique, sont semblables et partagent des solutions sans jamais se répéter, une évolution étant sans cesse perceptible.

Ses édifices sont, outre pratiques, d'une beauté indiscutable, reposant plus qu'à son tour sur la simplicité des éléments et une certaine approche de la sobriété. Mais c'est lors de son étape vénitienne et pour ses projets religieux qu'il exploite le plus ces caractéristiques : San Giorgio Maggiore et Il Redentore.

Palladio devient l'architecte qui comprend le mieux la noblesse vicentine, ayant abandonné le commerce pour la propriété foncière, et construit pour elle des maisons pratiques, commodes et saines avec des matériaux économiques. Cette mentalité présente des similitudes avec celle de la noblesse anglaise et sa culture des cottages, mais aussi avec celle des grands propriétaires nord-américains, pragmatiques tout en demeurant amoureux de la monumentalité palladienne et de son apparence classique. Les caractéristiques propres à la société anglo-saxonne liées au succès des « Quattro Libri » de Palladio et au fait que Venise fut à compter du XVIIIème siècle une référence pour l'Angleterre, expliquent le profond retentissement historique des œuvres de Palladio, l'architecte le plus copié de toute l'histoire.

Verso la metà del secolo XVI, i mercanti veneziani, in altri tempi onnipotenti, si rendono conto che la loro piccola Repubblica non poteva più competere con i grandi imperi europei. Essi costituiscono una classe nobile e cosmopolita, che, a causa della crisi sofferta dal Mediterraneo in seguito alla crescita del commercio atlantico, si trova ora a fronteggiare l'esigenza di cambiare il proprio modo di fare affari. Il nuovo approccio che decidono di adottare consiste nell'investire le proprie fortune nella terraferma. Si trasformano i fangosi campi della regione in aree adatte all'agricoltura, mentre i mercanti, pur senza dimenticare le proprie origini nobili ed urbane, si trasferiscono dalle città alle campagne per poter dirigere personalmente i raccolti. Da ciò consegue che si renda necessaria una nuova architettura, non solo funzionale al lavoro agricolo, ma in grado anche di tenere in considerazione il fatto che i suoi utenti non sono contadini, bensì nobili che provengono dalla città. Inoltre, a fronte del delicato momento economico in cui ci si trova, è necessario che queste costruzioni possano edificarsi per fasi, a seconda della liquidità a disposizione del proprietario.

È in questo contesto che fa la propria apparizione Andrea di Pietro della Gondola, altrimenti detto Palladio dal suo mentore Giangiorgio Trissino, il più importante intellettuale di Vicenza, una delle città che rendevano tributo a Venezia. È proprio questo umanista che scopre il trentenne scalpellino Andrea di Pietro e gli imparte un'edu-

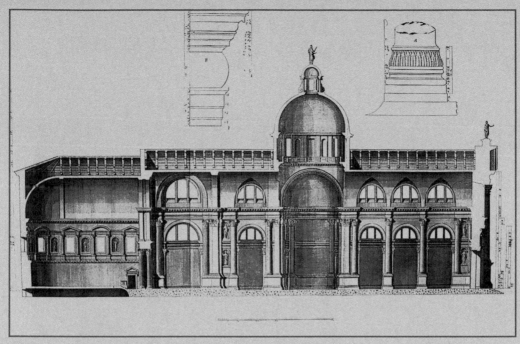

Church of the Convent of San Giorgio Maggiore

cazione classica dopo aver provato la sua predisposizione all'apprendimento e la sua inclinazione per gli studi matematici.

La formazione quindi che Andrea riceve è quella del tecnico con nozioni più o meno solide di umanista, piuttosto che quella dell'umanista propriamente detto. Conosce i testi di Vitruvio e dell'Alberti, ma lui è un architetto pratico e non teorico, come ben dimostra nei suoi "Quattro Libri" (Venezia 1570), dove si preoccupa più di soluzioni pragmatiche che dei problemi teorici dell'Architettura.

Palladio dimostra una versatilità sorprendente. Tutte le sue ville appartengono alla medesima famiglia architettonica: prendono avvio da un corpo principale quadrato, senza cortile centrale e quasi sempre con le tipiche brachese laterali (portici per gli attrezzi dell'agricoltura), ma ognuna è adattata alle esigenze specifiche di cada proprietario. Tutti gli studi condotti nel XX° secolo mettono in evidenza questo aspetto singolare dell'architetto di Vicenza. Sembra che Palladio abbia uno schema mentale molto chiaro delle esigenze di questo tipo di edificio e che vada adeguando questo modello ideale alle contingenze del preventivo, del terreno e delle funzioni specifiche, che deve alloggiare. In ogni caso, non si tratta di un idealismo, quanto piuttosto di un'idea modulare dell'architettura: Palladio progetta partendo da pezzi differenti appartenenti ad un repertorio limitato che possono combinarsi tra di loro in infinite combinazioni. Probabil-

mente, da questo punto di vista, l'elemento più evidente è costituito dagli accessi principali: tutti devono la propria origine all'idea del frontone classico, sono simili e condividono alcune soluzioni, ma non ce n'è nessuno che si ripeta, sempre è apprezzabile un'evoluzione.

I suoi edifici sono, oltre che pratici, di una bellezza indiscutibile, fondata molto spesso nella semplicità dei suoi elementi ed in un assai sofisticato concetto di sobrietà. Dove però maggiormente si esprimono questi caratteri è nella tappa veneziana e nei progetti religiosi: San Giorgio Maggiore e il Redentore.

Palladio si presenta come l'architetto che ha compreso la nobiltà vicentina nel suo passaggio dal mondo mercantile a quello del latifondo e per essa progetta case pratiche, comode, ben fatte e con materiali economici. Questa mentalità presenta delle similitudini con quella dei nobili inglesi e la loro cultura dei cottages, ed anche con quella dei grandi proprietari nordamericani, pragmatici ed al tempo stesso amanti della monumentalità palladiana e del suo aspetto classico. Le caratteristiche proprie della società anglosàssone, insieme al grande successo che ebbero i "Quattro Libri" ed al fatto che Venezia divenne dal XVIII° secolo un referente per l'Inghilterra, spiegano l'enorme fortuna critica delle opere di Palladio, l'architetto più copiato della storia.

Palladian Basilica

Piazza dei Signori, Vicenza, Italy
1546–1549

The basilica was Palladio's first public building, commissioned by Vicenza's Council of Five Hundred. It is in fact a structure that surrounds a pre-existing Gothic building with the intention of shoring it up and embellishing it. The new classical idiom had to disguise some irregularly shaped galleries and the huge pillars on the corners, while adapting to the dimensions of the original building – its great breadth, its height spanning two stories and its trapezoidal layout. Palladio managed to achieve a sense of unity in the façades by using a repeated module on both stories; the regularity of its elements hides the lack of symmetry in the internal structure. This module – known even today as a Palladian arch or motif, even though it was invented by Bramante and popularized by Serlio – comprises an arch and lintel supported not by a wall but by pillars. The sheer elegance of the building, with its striking chiaroscuros, prevents visitors from noticing its – admittedly minimal – lack of symmetry, while the imposing ceiling stylizes the whole structure and emphasizes the upward thrust of the pillars topped with sculptures.

Die Basilika ist das erste öffentliche Bauwerk Palladios und wurde vom Rat der Fünfhundert von Vicenza in Auftrag gegeben. Die Aufgabe bestand darin, eine Struktur zu schaffen, die ein bereits bestehendes gotisches Gebäude abstützen und verschönern sollte. Die neue klassische Formensprache musste die riesigen Eckpfeiler und unregelmäßigen Korridore verbergen sowie sich maßlich der Breite, der Höhe von zwei Stockwerken und dem trapezförmigen Grundriss des bereits vorhandenen Gebäudes anpassen. Die Lösung für das einheitliche Aussehen der Fassaden besteht in einem in beiden Geschossen wiederholten Modul, der durch die Regelmäßigkeit seiner Bestandteile die fehlende Symmetrie der inneren Struktur überdeckt. Dieser Modul wurde zwar von Bramante erfunden und von Serlio verbreitet, ist jedoch noch heute als palladianischer Bogen oder palladianisches Motiv bekannt. Der Bogen folgt hierbei auf den Fenstersturz, der nicht von einer Mauer, sondern von Säulen gestützt wird. Die Eleganz des Gebäudes mit ihrem wirkungsvollen Hell-Dunkel-Kontrast verhindert, dass der Betrachter den tatsächlich vorhandenen, minimalen Mangel an Symmetrie bemerkt. Das mächtige Dach verleiht dem gesamten Volumen seinen Stil und verstärkt die vertikale Linie, die von den mit Skulpturen gekrönten Säulen vorgegeben wird.

La basilique constitue la première œuvre publique de cet architecte et lui fut commandée par le Conseil des Cinq-Cents de Vicenza. Le projet est, en fait, une structure qui ceint une construction gothique pré-existante conçue afin de l'étayer et de l'embellir. Le nouveau langage classique devait dissimuler les énormes piliers de chaque coin et des espaces irréguliers tout en s'adaptant aux dimensions de la construction précédente : la largeur, la hauteur des niveaux et l'étage trapézoïdal. La solution pour obtenir une sensation d'unité des façades passe par un module répété sur les deux niveaux qui, de par la régularité de ses éléments, arrive à dissimuler le manque de symétrie de la structure interne. Dans ce module, encore connu comme arche ou motif palladien, bien qu'inventé par Bramante et popularisé par Serlio, se succèdent l'arche et un linteau soutenus non par un mur mais par des colonnes. L'élégance de l'édifice, affichant un puissant jeu de clairs-obscurs, évite que le spectateur ne prenne conscience de la symétrie, en fait minime, alors que la couverte solide stylise tout le volume en renforçant la verticalité imprimée par les colonnes couronnées de sculptures.

La basilica è la prima opera pubblica di questo architetto e gli venne commissionata dal Consiglio dei Cinquecento di Vicenza. Il progetto è in realtà una struttura che circonda un edificio gotico preesistente, disegnata con l'obiettivo di puntellarlo e migliorarne l'aspetto. Il nuovo linguaggio classico doveva dissimulare gli enormi pilastri degli angoli ed alcune corsie irregolari ed adattarsi alle misure dell'edificio precedente: la larghezza, l'altezza di due piani e la pianta trapezoidale. La soluzione adottata per ottenere la sensazione di unitarietà nelle facciate si basò in un modulo ripetuto su entrambi i piani che, grazie alla regolarità dei propri elementi, riesce a nascondere la mancanza di simmetria della struttura interna. In questo modulo – che ancor oggi si conosce come arco o motivo palladiano, anche se lo codificò il Bramante e lo rese popolare il Serlio – si succedono un arco ed una piattabanda non sostenuti da un muro, bensì appoggiati a delle colonne. L'eleganza dell'edificio, dotato di un potente gioco di chiaroscuri, evita che l'osservatore si renda conto della mancanza – per la verità, minima – di simmetria, mentre la grande copertura stilizza tutto il volume rafforzandone la verticalità impressa dalle colonne coronate da sculture.

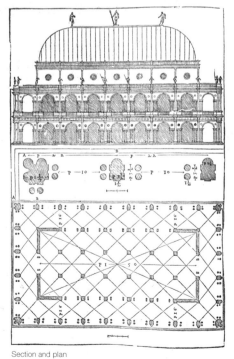

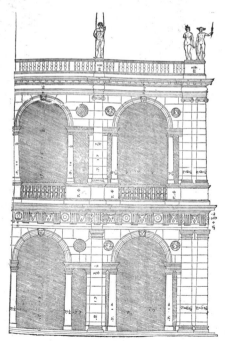

Section and plan
Schnitt und Grundriss
Section et niveau
Sezione e pianta

 0 4 8

Elevation
Aufriss
Elévation
Prospetto

0 1 2

Palazzo Chiericati

Piazza Matteotti, Vicenza, Italy
1550

In this palace, commissioned by one of the supervisors of the Palladian Basilica, Andrea Palladio rejected the Roman model, with its living quarters spread round an inner courtyard in favor of that of the palaces of Vicenza, which open onto the street. The Palazzo Chiericati looks onto a square and its sides are unencumbered by other buildings, which means that it can be seen in perspective. The low façade runs along the street and, in keeping with the tradition in Vicenza, incorporates a portico that provides shelter for passers-by. The division of the building into three vertical units counteracts any possible monotony on the horizontal plane and very concisely emphasizes both the symmetry and the main entrance under the second floor of the central unit. A group of statues stands on the cornice, in line with the pillars which prolong the building's vertical axis, preventing it from looking too squat. Palladio used this kind of design – similar to that of a villa – for palaces in squares or wide avenues where the façade can be viewed as a whole, while in narrow streets, where the plots were normally longer, he preferred to build courtyards and a façade with fewer elements.

Dieser Palast war der Auftrag einer der Aufseher der Basilica. Bei ihm vermied Andrea Palladio das römische Schema, bei dem das Haus um einen Innenhof herum gebaut wird, und zog stattdessen das Schema von Vicenza des nach der Straße hin offenen Palastes vor. Der Palazzo Chiericati erhebt sich an einem Platz und an seinen Flanken befinden sich keine anderen Gebäuden, so dass eine perspektivische Ansicht möglich ist. Die Fassade entwickelt sich parallel zur Straße und folgt so der vicentinischen Tradition eines Säulenganges zum Schutz der Passanten. Die Aufteilung in drei vertikale Körper wirkt einer möglichen horizontalen Monotonie entgegen und betont auf sehr einfache Weise die Symmetrie sowie den Haupteingang, der sich unter dem mittleren Körper des zweiten Stockwerks befindet. Auf dem Gesims befindet sich eine Reihe von an den Säulen ausgerichteten Statuen, die die senkrechte Linie des Gebäudes fortsetzen und einen Ausgleich zur horizontalen Struktur bilden. Diese Gestaltung eines Palastes, die eher der einer Villa ähnelt, setzt Palladio bei breiten Chausseen oder Plätzen ein, die eine frontale Ansicht ermöglichen. Im Falle von engen Straßen, an denen normalerweise längliche Grundstücke liegen, zieht er Bauten mit Innenhöfen und einer Fassade ohne viele Volumen vor.

Pour ce palais commandé par l'un des superviseurs de la Basilique Palladienne, Andrea Palladio se détourna du concept romain, qui sous-tendait la maison construite autour d'un patio intérieur, pour suivre le schéma vicentin du palais ouvert sur la route. Le Palazzo Chiericati s'élève devant une place et ses flancs demeurent libres de toute autre construction, offrant une vue en perspective. La façade se développe parallèlement à la rue, suivant la tradition vicentine du portique couvrant les passants. La division en trois corps verticaux contrebalance la possible monotonie horizontale et marque très simplement la symétrie et l'accès principal, sous le corps central du deuxième étage. Sur la corniche, des statues se dressent en groupe, alignées avec les colonnes, prolongeant la verticalité de l'édifice et offrant un pendant à sa verticalité. La conception de ce palais, plus semblable à celui d'une villa, est utilisée par Palladio dans de larges avenues ou sur des places proposant une vision frontale. En revanche, il préfère, pour les rues étroites normalement plus en longueur, recourir aux patios et aux façades avec moins de volumes.

In questo palazzo commissionato da uno dei supervisori della Basilica Palladiana, Andrea Palladio abbandonò lo schema romano, in cui l'abitazione si organizza attorno ad un patio centrale, per adottare invece lo schema vicentino del palazzo aperto verso la strada. Palazzo Chiericati si innalza di fronte ad una piazza ed i suoi fianchi sono liberi da altre edificazioni, la qual cosa permette che l'edificio possa essere visto in prospettiva. La facciata si sviluppa parallelamente alla strada, seguendo la tradizione vicentina di creare un portico con cui proteggere i passanti. La divisione in tre corpi verticali si contrappone alla possibile monotonia orizzontale e marca in modo semplice la simmetria e l'accesso principale sotto il corpo principale del secondo piano. Al di sopra della cornice si eleva un gruppo di statue allineate alle colonne che prolungano la verticalità dell'edificio interrompendone l'orizzontalità. Questo tipo di palazzo, più simile alla villa, Palladio lo utilizza in strade ampie o piazze che consentano una visione frontale, mentre nelle vie strette ed in presenza normalmente di lotti più allungati, preferisce la costruzione di patii e di una facciata senza tanti volumi.

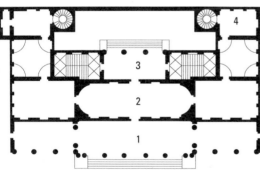

Plan
Grundriss
Niveau
Pianta

1. Access
2. Hall
3. Access to superior floors

1. Eingang
2. Diele
3. Zugang den oberen Etagen

1. Accès
2. Vestibule
3. Accés aux étages superieurs

1. Entrata
2. Ingresso
3. Accesso ai piani superiori

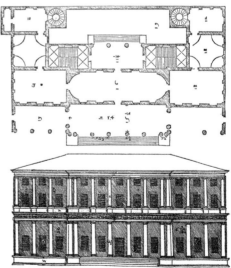

Elevation and plan
Aufriss und Grundriss
Élevation et niveau
Prospetto e pianta

 0 5 10

Elevation
Aufriss
Élévation
Prospetto

0 1 2

Church of the Convent of San Giorgio Maggiore

Canale della Giudecca, Venice, Italy
1560–1565

San Giorgio was the first church entirely designed by Palladio, and it is one of Venice's most famous buildings, largely due to its exceptional location in the monastic complex on the island of San Giorgio. Palladio came up with a façade that juxtaposes two classical temples to adapt the classical proportions to the basilical model, where the central nave is higher than the side ones – unthinkable in a classical temple. The central pediment is the dominant element of the whole composition, while the half-pediments rest on pilasters that rise directly from the floor, in contrast with the half-pillars of the central order, which are raised on tall pedestals. Palladio tried to reflect the demarcations inside the building on the façade, and so he emphasized the part of the façade corresponding to the longitudinal axis of the central nave. Inside, the choir – an area set apart behind the altar – is unusual, with a design anticipating the structure of Il Redentore. Palladio was confronted with the complex problems thrown up by the Renaissance, such as the nature of a Christian place of worship. Although he was removed from the architectural centers in which these issues had arisen – or precisely because of this – Palladio opted for functionalism and a very clear language.

San Giorgio war die erste vollständig von Palladio entworfene Kirche. Sie ist aufgrund ihrer privilegierten Lage im klösterlichen Komplex der Insel San Giorgio eines der bekanntesten Gebäude in Venedig. Die Lösung des Baumeisters für die Fassade bestand im Nebeneinandersetzen zweier Kirchen. Auf diese Weise passte er die klassischen Proportionen an die Vertikalprojektion einer Basilika an, bei der das Mittelschiff höher als die Seitenschiffe ist, was bei einem klassischen Tempel undenkbar wäre. Der zentrale Giebel ist das die ganze Komposition beherrschende Element. Die Halbgiebel hingegen ruhen auf direkt vom Boden ausgehenden Wandpfeilern, die einen Kontrast zu den auf hohen Sockeln errichteten Halbsäulen des zentralen Blockes bilden. Das Ansinnen Palladios ist die Übertragung der Hierarchie des Inneren des Gebäudes auf die Fassade. Aus diesem Grund betont er den Teil der Fassade, der der Längsachse des Mittelschiffs entspricht. Im Inneren überrascht der Chor hinter dem Hochaltar, ein gesonderter Raum, der bereits die Struktur von Il Redentore vorwegnimmt. Palladio ist mit den während der Renaissance aufgeworfenen komplexen Problemen wie beispielsweise der Typologie der christlichen Kirchen konfrontiert. Obwohl er sich weit entfernt von den Zentren der Baukunst befand, in denen diese Fragen aufgekommen waren – oder vielleicht gerade deshalb –, entschied er sich für Funktionalität und eine sehr klare Sprache.

San Giorgio fut la première église projetée entièrement par Palladio. Elle constitue l'un des édifices vénitiens les plus connu de par sa situation privilégiée, dans l'ensemble monastique de l'île de San Giorgio. L'architecte résolut la façade en juxtaposant deux temples afin d'adapter les proportions classiques au niveau basilical, où la nef centrale est plus haute que les latérales, impensable pour un temple classique. Le fronton central est l'élément qui domine toute la composition, alors que les frontons reposent sur des pilastres jaillissant directement du sol et contrastant avec les demi-colonnes de l'ordre central, posées sur de hauts piédestaux. Palladio a cherché à transmettre, grâce à la façade, les hiérarchies de l'intérieur de l'édifice. De ce fait, il porte l'accent sur la partie de la façade correspondant à l'axe longitudinal de la nef centrale. À l'intérieur, le chœur surprend, derrière l'autel principal, un lieu à part qui annonce déjà la structure d'Il Redentore. Palladio s'affronte aux problèmes complexes posés par la Renaissance, ainsi la typologie du temple chrétien. Bien qu'à l'écart des centres architecturaux où se développèrent ces thèmes, il opta pour le fonctionnalisme et pour la clarté du langage.

San Giorgio fu la prima chiesa progettata interamente dal Palladio e costituisce uno degli edifici veneziani più conosciuti per effetto della sua posizione, nel complesso dell'isola di San Giorgio. L'architetto risolse la facciata attraverso la giustapposizione di due templi, per poter adattare le proporzioni classiche all'alzato basilicare, dove la navata centrale è più alta di quelle laterali (cosa questa impensabile in un tempio classico). Il frontone centrale è l'elemento che domina tutta la composizione, mentre i mezzi frontoni riposano su alcuni pilastri che si innalzano direttamente dal suolo e che contrastano con le semi-colonne dell'ordine centrale appoggiate sopra alti piedistalli. Palladio cerca di trasmettere nella facciata le gerarchie dell'interiore dell'edificio e per questo enfatizza la parte di facciata che corrisponde all'asse longitudinale della navata centrale. Dell'interno stacca, dietro all'altare maggiore, il coro, un ambito a parte che già guarda alla struttura del Redentore. Palladio si confronta con i problemi che il Rinascimento aveva posto sul tavolo, come la tipologia del tempio cristiano. Sebbene lontano dai centri architettonici in cui si erano andate sviluppando queste discussioni, o forse proprio per questa ragione, egli optò per il funzionalismo.

26 Church of the Convent of San Giorgio Maggiore

28 Church of the Convent of San Giorgio Maggiore

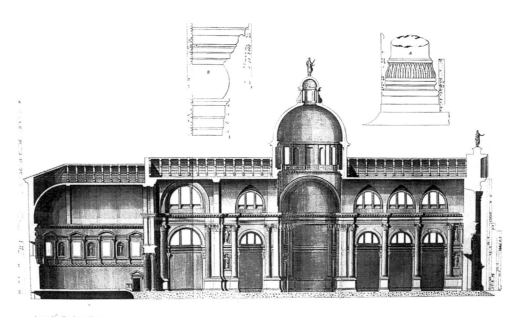

Longitudinal section
Längsschnitt
Section longitudinale
Sezione longitudinale

0 4 8

Elevation
Aufriss
Élévation
Prospetto

0 2 4

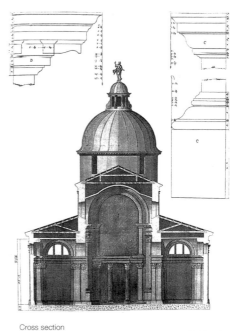

Cross section
Querschnitt
Section perpendiculaire
Sezione transversale

0 2 4

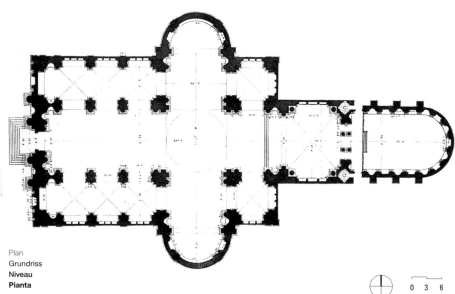

Plan
Grundriss
Niveau
Pianta

⊕ 0 3 6

Church of Il Redentore

Canale della Giudecca, Venice, Italy
1576–1577

The Church of Il Redentore was a gift to the Capuchin order from the senators of Venice, in fulfilment of a vow made to deliver the city from the plague of 1575. For this reason it had to serve three different functions: the order's monastic function in the chorus, behind a row of columns; the votive one, at the altar, and the congregational one, in the chapels. The central nave receives the very diffuse light that enters through the thermal windows before being gently filtered by the matt stucco of the vault. The altar, situated under the cupola, is more brightly lit, although less so than the choir, where the sunlight pours in through the low windows and sparkles on the glossy stucco. This graduation, which is also reflected in the layout – the three areas are on slightly separate levels – enhances the longitudinal thrust towards the altar, which unifies the three different sections. The façade evokes a classical temple; by pushing the half pediments on the side back onto a deeper plane, Palladio emphasized the main tympanum, with its half-pillars and pilasters, while the succession of elements in depth gives cohesion to the whole building around the cupola.

Die Kirche Il Redentore ist eine Spende der Senatoren Venedigs an den Kapuzinerorden in Erfüllung eines Gelübdes, das die Stadt 1575 von der Pest befreien sollte. Daher musste sie gleichzeitig drei unterschiedliche Funktionen erfüllen: die klösterliche des Ordens im Chor hinter einer Säulenreihe, die eines Votivraumes in Form des Altars und die glaubensgemeinschaftliche in den Kapellen. Das Mittelschiff ist in ein sehr diffuses Licht getaucht, das durch die Thermenfenster einfällt und durch das matte Stuckwerk des Gewölbes leicht absorbiert wird. Der unter der Kuppel befindliche Altar ist wesentlich besser beleuchtet und kontrastiert mit dem Chor, dessen Licht, das durch niedrige Fenster einfällt, dank des glatten Steins sehr hell ist. So entsteht eine Abstufung bezüglich des Lichtes und der Baukörper, die zu leicht unterschiedlichen Ebenen der drei Räume führt. In der Längsrichtung hingegen strebt alles verstärkt dem Altar zu und führt so die drei unterschiedlichen Teilbereiche wieder zusammen. Die Fassade betont das Erscheinungsbild des klassischen Tempels. Indem die seitlichen Halbgiebel auf eine tiefere Ebene herabgezogen werden, hebt sich der Haupttympanon mit seinen Halb- und Wandsäulen hervor, während die Abfolge der Elemente in der Tiefe das gesamte Bauwerk um die Kuppel herum anordnet.

L'église d'Il Redentore est une donation des sénateurs de Venise à l'ordre des Capucins suite à la réalisation d'un vœux devant libérer la ville de la peste en 1575. Elle devait, de ce fait, réunir trois fonctions distinctes : la monastique de l'ordre, dans le chœur, derrière un alignement de colonnes, la votive, en autel, et la congrégationnelle, dans les chapelles. La nef centrale jouit d'une lumière particulièrement diffuse s'infiltrant par les fenêtres thermales et légèrement tamisée par le stuc mat de la voûte. L'autel, situé sous la coupole, est suffisamment illuminé et contraste avec le chœur, dont la lumière, très brillante en raison du stuc lisse, pénètre par les fenêtres basses. De légères différences de niveau étant patentes entre les trois espaces, cette gradation lumineuse et physique donne force à la direction longitudinale vers l'autel, ce qui insuffle une certaine cohérence aux trois parties. La façade accentue l'apparence de temple classique, en retirant vers un plan plus profond les frontons latéraux moyens, mettant en exergue le tympan principal et ses colonnes et pilastres moyens, alors que la succession d'éléments en profondeur renforce la cohésion de l'édifice autour de la coupole.

La chiesa del **Redentore** è una donazione del Senato di Venezia all'Ordine dei Cappuccini, in adempimento ad un voto che aveva liberato la città dalla peste del 1575. Per questa ragione, doveva riunire tre distinte funzioni: quella monastica dell'Ordine nel coro, dietro ad una fila di colonne, quella votiva nell'altare e quella congregazionale nelle cappelle. La navata centrale gode di una luce diafana che entra attraverso i finestroni termali e che è leggermente mediata dall'effetto del trattamento mate della cupola. L'altare, situato sotto la cupola, è abbastanza più illuminato e contrasta con il coro, la cui luce, molto brillante grazie allo stucco liscio, entra attraverso delle finestre basse. Con questa differenziazione luminosa e fisica – vi sono piccoli cambi di quota tra i tre spazi – si potenzia la direzionalità longitudinale verso l'altare, cosa che rende coerente le differenze tra i tre ambiti. La facciata accentua l'aspetto di tempio classico; collocando in un piano più arretrato i medi frontoni laterali, risalta il timpano principale, le sue medie colonne ed il pilastri, mentre la successione di elementi in profondità coesivo tutto l'edificio attorno alla sua cupola.

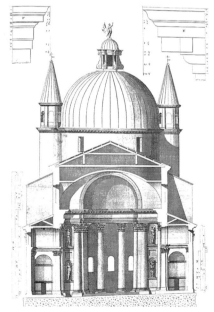

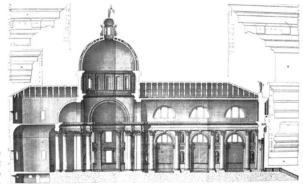

Longitudinal section
Längsschnitt
Section longitudinale
Sezione longitudinale

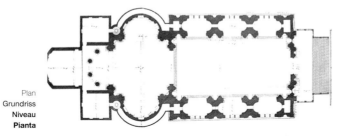

Plan
Grundriss
Niveau
Pianta

0 4 8

Olympic Theater

Piazza Matteotti, Vicenza, Italy
1579–1580

When Daniele Barbaro produced an edition of the work of Vitruvius in 1556, he included a series of drawings of theaters which may possibly have come from the pen of Palladio. In the years to come, the artist was to build at least three theaters, but the structure of this theater is far removed from the innovations that were spreading all over Italy at that time. In 1579 the Olympic Academy decided to build a permanent theater; the Commune donated a piece of land for this purpose but, as it lay between other buildings, it was impossible to build a façade. The construction work began in February 1580, according to a model made by Palladio, and was almost finished when the architect died the following August. Palladio was always interested in archeology as, along with Vitruvius' text, it was the only contemporary source to which the architects of his time had access. However, it was an interest that served his training in adapting classical structures to the functions of his age without ever embodying any desire to rebuild the past per se.

Als Daniele Barbaro 1556 eine Ausgabe des Werkes von Vitruv erstellte, nahm er auch eine Reihe von Zeichnungen von Theatern darin auf, die möglicherweise von Palladio angefertigt worden waren. In den darauf folgenden Jahren baute Andrea Palladio mindestens drei Theater im klassischen Stil. Er befand sich damit sehr weit von den Erneuerungen entfernt, die sich über ganz Italien ausbreiteten und die in die Struktur dieses Bauwerkes, so wie wir es heute kennen, münden sollten. Im Jahre 1579 beschloss die Olympische Akademie den Bau eines festen Theaters. Die Comuna trat hierfür ein Grundstück ab, auf dem aber keine Fassade errichtet werden konnte, da es sich zwischen anderen Gebäuden befand. Die Bauarbeiten begannen im Februar 1580 nach einem Modell von Palladio und waren fast beendet, als der Baumeister im August starb. Palladio hegte immer großes Interesse für Archäologie, da diese zusammen mit dem Text Vitruvs die einzige alte Quelle war, aus der die Architekten seiner Epoche lernen konnten. Dies war aber ein rein auf seine Ausbildung gerichtetes Interesse, um die klassischen Strukturen an die Funktionen seiner Zeit anzupassen, und niemals ein Versuch, die Vergangenheit um ihrer selbst Willen zu rekonstruieren.

Lorsqu'en 1556 Daniele Barbaro termine une édition de l'œuvre de Vitruve, il y inclut une série de dessins de théâtres probablement réalisés par Palladio. Avec la succession des années, l'artiste construisit pour le moins trois théâtres suivant les schémas classiques, très éloignés des innovations qui se propageaient dans toute l'Italie et qui mèneraient à la structure de cette construction telle qu'elle nous est parvenue. En 1579, l'Académie Olympique décida de construire un théâtre permanent et la Commune céda dans cette optique un terrain qui, situé entre d'autres édifices, empêchait la réalisation d'une façade. L'œuvre commença en février 1580, selon une maquette de Palladio, pour être quasiment achevées en août, à la mort de l'architecte. Palladio fut sans cesse intéressé par l'archéologie car, avec le texte de Vitruve, il s'agissait de la seule source antique de connaissance pour l'apprentissage des architectes de l'époque. Mais ce fut pour lui un intérêt tout à sa formation, afin d'adapter les structures classiques aux fonctions de l'époque et jamais une tentative de ressusciter le passé en soi.

Quando nel 1556 Daniele Barbaro portò a termine un'edizione dell'Opera di Vitruvio, incluse una serie di disegni di teatri che forse erano stati realizzati da Palladio. Negli anni successivi, l'artista costruì almeno tre teatri seguendo schemi classici, assai distanti dalle innovazioni che si stavano diffondendo in tutta Italia e che avrebbero portato alla tipologia come noi oggi la conosciamo. Nel 1579 l'Accademia Olimpica decise di costruire un teatro permanente; il Comune a tal fine le diede un lotto di terreno che, chiuso tra altri edifici, impedì la costruzione di una facciata. I lavori incominciarono nel Febbraio del 1580 su un modello del Palladio e stavano quasi teminati in Agosto, quando l'architetto morì. Palladio si interessò sempre di archeologia, visto che, insieme al testo di Vitruvio, era la unica fonte antica da cui potessero apprendere gli architetti dell'epoca. Questo suo interesse fu però chiaramente finalizzato solo alla sua formazione, per adeguare le strutture classiche alle funzioni della sua epoca, e mai alimentato da un intento di ricostruzione del passato quale processo fine a sé stesso.

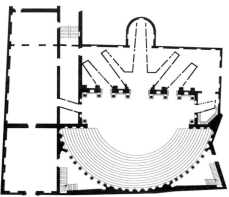

Cross section
Querschnitt
Section perpendiculaire
Sezione transversale

0 4 8

Plan
Grundriss
Niveau
Pianta

0 5 10

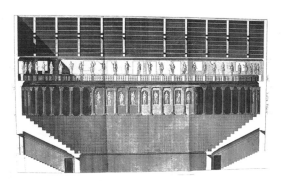

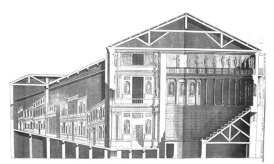

Cross section
Querschnitt
Section perpendiculaire
Sezione transversale

Longitudinal section
Längsschnitt
Section longitudinale
Sezione longitudinale

0   5   10

Villa Cornaro

Via Roma, Piombino Dese, Padua, Italy
1552

In his villas, Palladio adapted the pre-existing models to the needs of each client; this is why his villas seem to form a series. Nevertheless, the end results are always designed to satisfy a specific requirement, and it is this specificity which makes each one unique. The Villa Cornaro is basically a compact block with two side wings. The main body of the building revolves around the central hall. This central focus is balanced by a longitudinal axis joining the front and back façades, each of which has direct access onto the hall. The wings trace another longitudinal axis, perpendicular to the first, and in perfect counterpoint to it. On the exterior, the porticos of the two entrances stand out, as they are lower than the rest of the building, as well as being highly decorated and set off by their staircases. The portico on the front façade projects towards the exterior of the building, like a classical pronaos. This simple device bestows nobility on the whole building even though neither the windows nor the doors display any decoration.

Bei den Villen passt Palladio bereits vorhandene Modelle an die Bedürfnisse seines jeweiligen Kunden an, weshalb diese Bauten einen gewissen Beigeschmack von Serienhaftigkeit haben. Dennoch ist jede seiner Lösungen auf der Grundlage eines konkreten Bedürfnisses entworfen und es ist genau diese Besonderheit, die sie einzigartig macht. Die Villa Cornaro besteht aus einem kompakten Block mit zwei Seitenflügeln. Der Hauptkörper des Gebäudes bewegt sich um den mittleren Raum. Diese Ausrichtung auf das Zentrum hin wird durch eine Längsachse ausgeglichen, die von der vorderen und hinteren Fassade vorgegeben ist, und von denen aus ein direkter Zugang zum Raum besteht. Die Seitenflügel zeichnen eine weitere Längsachse senkrecht zur ersten und bilden einen perfekten Kontrapunkt zu dieser. Im Außenbereich, der tiefer liegt als der Rest des Gebäudes, stechen die Säulengänge der beiden Eingänge hervor, die üppig verziert und durch die beiden Zugangstreppen betont sind. Der Portikus an der vorderen Fassade projiziert sich wie ein klassischer Pronaos auf das Äußere des Gebäudes. Mit dieser simplen Lösung wird ein Komplex von edlem Erscheinungsbild geschaffen, obwohl weder Fenster noch Türen in irgendeiner Weise verziert sind.

Pour les villas, Palladio adapte les modèles pré-existants aux nécessités de chacun de ses clients, tout en préservant une certaine connotation sérielle. Pour autant, chacune de ses solutions est conçue à partir d'un besoin concret. C'est cette particularité qui les rend précisément uniques. La Villa Cornaro apparaît comme un bloc compact doté de deux ailes latérales. Le corps principal de la construction gravite autour de la salle centrale. Cette centralité est compensée par un axe longitudinal marqué par les façades avant et arrière, qui offrent un accès direct à la salle. Les ailes latérales dessinent un autre axe longitudinal, perpendiculaire au premier, et se comportent en parfait contrepoint. À l'extérieur, les portiques des deux entrées, plus bas que le reste de l'édifice, sont mis en avant, de par leur riche décoration et l'accent apporté par les escaliers d'accès. Le portique de la façade avant se projette vers l'extérieur, tel un pronaos classique. Avec cette solution simple, il peut créer un ensemble à l'apparence noble malgré le dépouillement décoratif des fenêtres et des portes.

Nelle ville, Palladio adatta i modelli preesistenti alle necessità di ognuno dei suoi clienti ed è per questa ragione le sue ville possiedono tale connotazione di serialità. Ognuna di queste soluzioni era comunque disegnata a partire da una necessità concreta ed è questo l'aspetto che le rende uniche. La villa Corsaro si articola come un blocco compatto con due ali laterali. Il corpo principale dell'edificio gravita attorno alla sala centrale. Questa centralità è compensata da un asse longitudinale marcato dalla facciata anteriore e posteriore, da cui si ha un accesso diretto alla sala. Le ali laterali disegnano un altro asse longitudinale perpendicolare la primo e funzionano da contrappunto. All'esterno, essendo più basse del resto dell'edificio, rialzano i portici delle due entrate, molto decorati ed enfatizzati dalla presenza degli scaloni d'accesso. Il portico della facciata principale si protende verso l'esterno come in un pronao classico. Con questa semplice soluzione si riesce ad ottenere un insieme di aspetto nobile nonostante il fatto che né le finestre, né le porte presentino decorazione alcuna.

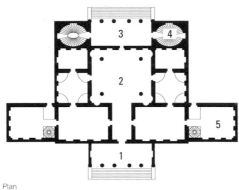

Plan
Grundriss
Niveau
Pianta

1. Access
2. Living room
3. Stairs

1. Accès
2. Salle de séjour
3. Escaliers

1. Eingang
2. Wohnzimmer
3. Treppe

1. Entrata
2. Salotto
3. Escala

Elevation   Élévation
Aufriss   **Prospetto**

0   3   6

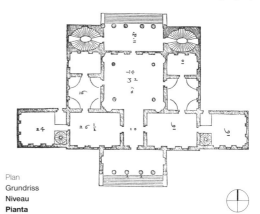

Plan
Grundriss
Niveau
Pianta

Villa Barbaro

Strada Comunale Bassanese, Maser, Treviso, Italy
1554

This villa in Maser was a working farmhouse, despite its lordly appearance. It was run by the Barbaro brothers, who lived in Venice. Daniele and Marcantonio had the benefits of a humanist education and studied in the University of Padua, as well as travelling to various foreign countries. They paid regular visits to Maser, not to escape the bustle of the city but to personally supervise the work on the land, as their fortune was dependent on the success of the harvest. The central (and most lordly) unit is set in front of the rest of the building so that it can benefit from the sunlight on three sides. The sides are broken by two porticos; these were used to store farming equipment or were even used as stables when necessary. The relationship between the different spaces is strictly hierarchical; the various sections are structured on a modular basis around a central unit, with a classical tympanum, which is the highest element - and the most voluminous, standing out from the rest of the façade. Paolo Veronese decorated the elegant interior between 1560 and 1562; this was the only collaboration between these two masters, and the result was a vibrant setting typical of Venice at that time.

Diese Villa in Maser fungierte trotz ihres herrschaftlichen Erscheinungsbildes als Bauernhof. Sie war der landwirtschaftliche Betrieb der Gebrüder Barbaro, die in Venedig lebten. Daniele und Marcantonio genossen eine humanistische Ausbildung, studierten an der Universität von Padua, und bereisten zudem verschiedene Länder. Sie kamen regelmässig nach Maser und dies nicht etwa, um dem Leben in der umtriebigen Stadt zu entfliehen, sondern um persönlich die Arbeiten auf dem Land zu leiten, da ihr Vermögen ja schließlich vom Erfolg der Ernte abhing. Der zentrale und zugleich herrschaftlichste Körper schiebt sich vor den Rest des Gebäudes, um so von drei Seiten Sonne zu haben. An den Flanken öffnen sich zwei Säulengänge, in denen die landwirtschaftlichen Geräte aufbewahrt wurden und die, wenn es nötig war, als Stall dienten. Die Beziehung zwischen diesen Räumen ist absolut hierarchisch. Die verschiedenen Teile gruppieren sich in Modulen um einen Zentralkörper. Dieser besitzt ein klassisches Tympanon und ist am höchsten und gewaltigsten, da er über den Rest der Fassade hinausragt. Paolo Veronese dekorierte zwischen 1560 und 1562 die edlen Innenräume des Hauses. Dies war das einzige Mal, dass die beiden Meister zusammen arbeiteten, um eine für das Umland Venedigs typische vibrierende Atmosphäre zu erschaffen.

Cette villa de Maser était une grange, en dépit de l'aspect seigneurial qu'elle offre. Elle constituait l'exploitation agricole des frères Barbaro, demeurant à Venise. Daniele et Marcantonio ont bénéficié d'une éducation humaniste et étudié à l'université de Padoue, tout en voyageant dans divers pays. Ils revenaient régulièrement à Maser, non pour s'éloigner de l'agitation de la vie citadine, mais plutôt pour diriger personnellement les travaux des champs, du succès de la récolte dépendant leur fortune. Le corps central, s'avance en regard du reste de l'édifice pour jouir de la lumière sur ses trois côtés. Deux portiques s'ouvrent sur ses flancs, afin d'héberger le harnachement pour le travail des champs ou servir d'étable, le cas échéant. La relation de ces deux espaces est absolument hiérarchique : les différentes parties se structurent de façon modulaire autour du corps central, avec un tympan classique, le plus haut et celui doté du volume le plus important, ressortant du reste de la façade. Paolo Veronese décora le noble intérieur de la demeure entre 1560 et 1562, ce qui constitue l'unique coopération entre ces deux maîtres afin de créer des atmosphères vivantes, typiques de l'environnement vénitien.

Questa villa del Maser funzionava come una casa contadina, nonostante l'aspetto signorile che la contraddistingueva. Era la tenuta agricola dei fratelli Barbaro, che vivevano a Venezia. Daniele e Marcantonio ebbero un'educazione umanista e studiarono all'Università di Padua, oltre a viaggiare attraverso molti paesi. Si recavano con regolarità al Maser non tanto per appartarsi dalla stressante vita cittadina, quanto piuttosto per dirigere personalmente i lavori nei campi, visto che la loro fortuna dipendeva dall'andamento del raccolto. Il corpo centrale, il più nobile, avanza rispetto al resto dell'edificio per poter disporre di luce sui tre lati. Ai suoi fianchi si aprono due portici, da dove si osservava l'attività nei campi o che venivano utilizzati come magazzino quando si rendesse necessario. La relazione di questi spazi era assolutamente gerarchica: le differenti parti si strutturano in forma modulare intorno ad un corpo centrale con un timpano classico, il più alto e quello che possiede il volume maggiore sporgendo dal reso della facciata. Paolo Veronese decorò gli interni della nobile dimora tra il 1560 e il 1562 in quella che fu l'unica occasione per questi due maestri di collaborare alla creazione delle atmosfere vivide tipiche dell'ambiente veneziano.

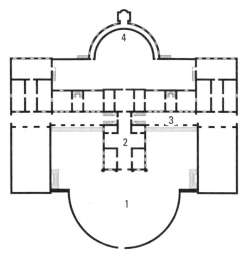

1. Courtyard
   Patio
   Cour
   Corte esterna
2. Living room
   Wohnzinmer
   Sala
   Stanza vivente

3. *Brachese*
   Brachese
   Brachese
   Brachese
4. Fountain
   Springbrunnen
   Fontaine
   Fontana

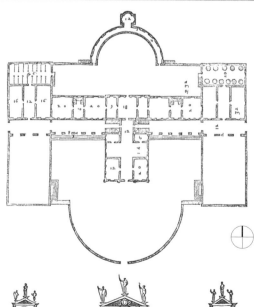

Elevation and plan **Élévation et niveau**
Aufriss und Grundriss **Prospetto e pianta**

0   5   10

Villa Badoer

Via T. Tasso 1, Fratta Polesine, Rovigo, Italy
1554

The Badoers were one of the wealthiest families in the region, and their villa shows off their economic status through its lavish interior decoration and the general impression of majestic elegance. Despite the amount of money that was obviously spent, Palladio's pragmatism is clearly apparent, the only ornamentation being the tympanum on the façade: the windows, with no pediments or any other decoration, are totally modern and would be unthinkable in Rome or Florence. Overall, the building follows the typical model for villas of this type, with a central unit for the owners and two side wings devoted to agricultural purposes. This project is distinctive as the side naves form a curve that opens onto a semicircular area in front of the main façade. An imposing staircase sets off the regal elegance of the façade, as well as constituting a transitional element between the villa itself and the working area; two side staircases directly connect the house with the two wings. The innovation of the two curved porticos, which reveal the freedom with which Palladio used the classical idiom, was greatly imitated in the eighteenth century.

Die Familie Badoer war eine der reichsten dieser Gegend. Ihre Villa zeugt von ihrer finanziellen Stellung durch die reichliche Innendekoration und die majestätische Eleganz des gesamten Komplexes. Trotz des offensichtlichen Reichtums kommt aber der pragmatische Geist Palladios deutlich zum Ausdruck, der außer des Tympanons der Fassade keine weiteren Ornamente verwenden wollte. Die Fenster ohne Giebel oder weitere Verzierungen sind absolut modern und wären so in Rom oder Florenz undenkbar gewesen. Der Komplex folgt dem für gleichartige Bauten typischen Schema und besteht aus einem Mittelkörper für die Eigentümer mit zwei Seitenflügeln für die landwirtschaftlichen Belange. Das Besondere an diesem Entwurf ist der gebogene Grundriss der Seitenschiffe, der einen halbkreisförmigen Raum vor der Hauptfassade öffnet. Eine imposante Treppe hebt das majestätische Aussehen der Fassade hervor und bildet außerdem ein Übergangselement zwischen der Villa selbst und dem Arbeitsbereich. Zwei Seitentreppen verbinden das Haus direkt mit den beiden Flügeln. Die Neuheit der beiden gebogenen Säulenvorbauten wurde im 18. Jahrhundert häufig nachgeahmt und ist ein Beweis für die Freiheit Palladios beim Verwenden klassischer Ausdrucksformen.

La famille Badoer était l'une des plus riches de la région, sa villa symbolisant la position économique qu'elle occupait grâce à une profusion de décorations intérieures et l'élégante majesté de l'ensemble. En dépit de son évidente richesse, le pragmatisme de Palladio ressurgit dans l'absence de recherche ornementale, hormis le tympan de la façade : les fenêtres sans fronton ou autre décoration, d'une modernité absolue, sont impensables à Rome ou à Florence. L'ensemble suit le plan typique des autres constructions de ce genre et se fonde sur un corps central destiné aux propriétaires, avec deux ailes dédiées aux fonctions agricoles. Ce projet a pour particularité ses nefs centrales présentant un niveau courbe, s'ouvrant sur un espace semi-circulaire devant la façade principale. Un escalier imposant rehausse la majesté de la façade et constitue, en outre, un élément transitionnel entre la villa proprement dite et la zone de travail ; deux escaliers latéraux connectent la maison directement avec ces deux ailes. L'innovation des deux portiques courbes fut très imitée au XVIIIème siècle et démontre la liberté de Palladio à l'heure de recourir au langage classique.

La famiglia Badoer era una delle più ricche della regione e la sua villa dimostra tale posizione economica attraverso una ricca decorazione negli interni e l'elegante maestosità dell'insieme. Nonostante la sua evidente ricchezza, si mostra radicale il pragmatismo palladiano al non ricercare alcun ornamento che andasse oltre il timpano della facciata: le finestre, senza frontoni o alcuna altra decorazione, di una modernità assoluta, erano impensabili nella Roma o Firenze dell'epoca. Il sistema segue la matrice tipica delle altre costruzioni del medesimo tipo e si basa in un corpo centrale per il proprietario con due ali laterali dedicate alle funzioni agricole. Questo progetto ha la peculiarità che le navate laterali adottano una pianta curva, per cui si apre uno spazio semicircolare di fronte alla facciata principale. Un'imponente scala accresce la maestosità della facciata e costituisce, in aggiunta, un elemento di transizione tra la villa propriamente detta e la zona di lavoro; due scale laterali connettono la casa direttamente con le due ali. L'innovazione dei due portici curvi venne molto imitata nel corso del XVIII° secolo e dimostra la libertà con cui il Palladio gestisse il linguaggio classico.

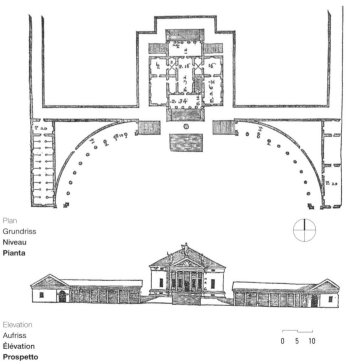

Plan
Grundriss
Niveau
Pianta

Elevation
Aufriss
Élévation
Prospetto

0   5   10

Villa Emo

Via Stazione 5, Fanzolo di Vedelago, Treviso, Italy
1558

Leonardo Emo's family had owned land in the Fanzolo area since the middle of the fourteenth century. This area had been deeply marked by the Romans, as can be seen from the remains of an old Roman road, and everything suggests that the division of the land dated back to the same period. The villa dominates all the surrounding area by being built on top of a base. The long straight road leading to the villa ends in a ramp that compensates for the elevation of the base and directly connects the main façade with the road in a very deep perspective that integrates the whole building into the landscape. Two brachese with a simple arcade were added to the sides of the main house to store the farming equipment, and these were topped off with two towers with dovecotes. These structures provide a frame for the mansion house, which follows the typical Palladian model. The entrance is a simple portico with Doric pillars, with no decoration on the door or the windows. The motif of the Doric capital is repeated, in simplified form, on the pillars in the side arcades. The interior was decorated by Battista Zelotti, who also worked on the Villa Godi and La Malcontenta.

Die Familie von Leonardo Emo besaß ab der Mitte des 14. Jahrhunderts Ländereien in der Ortschaft Fanzolo. Das Gebiet war ausgiebig romanisiert worden, wie am Verlauf einer antiken Römerstraße zu sehen ist, und alles weist darauf hin, dass die Parzellenaufteilung nach Modellen aus eben jener Epoche erfolgte. Die Villa beherrscht sämtliche Grundstücke in ihrem Umkreis, da sie auf einem Unterbau errichtet ist. Die lange und gerade Zugangsstraße endet in einer Rampe, die den durch den Unterbau entstehenden Höhenunterschied überbrückt, und verbindet die Hauptfassade direkt mit dem Weg in einer überaus langen Perspektive, die den Komplex in die Landschaft integriert. An den Seiten des Haupthauses wurden zwei brachese mit einem einfachen Bogen angefügt, die von zwei jeweils mit Taubenschlägen versehenen Türmen gekrönt sind. Diese Struktur rahmt das Herrschaftshaus ein, das dem palladianischen Schema mit quadratischem Grundriss folgt. Der Eingang ist ein einfacher Vorbau mit dorischen Säulen ohne jegliche Verzierung an Tür oder Fenstern. Das Motiv des dorischen Kapitels wiederholt sich in vereinfachter Form an den Pfeilern der seitlichen Bögen. Das Innere der Villa wurde von Battista Zelotti dekoriert, der auch an der Villa Godi und bei La Malcontenta mitgearbeitet hatte.

La famille de Leonardo Emo possédait des terres dans la ville de Fanzolo, depuis le milieu du XIVème siècle. Cette zone avait été profondément romanisée, comme le démontre le tracé d'une antique voie romaine, et tout indique que la parcellisation suivait les modèles de la même époque. La villa domine tous les terrains alentours, s'élevant sur une hauteur du terrain. Longue et rectiligne, la route d'accès à la villa culmine avec une rampe qui permet de passer le niveau du socle et connecte directement la façade principale avec le chemin, en une perspective amplissime intégrant l'ensemble dans le paysage. Sur les côtés de la demeure, deux brachese ont été ajoutés avec une arcade simple et couronnés de deux tours arborant toutes deux des colombiers. Cette structure encadre la maison noble, qui respecte le concept palladien des niveaux quadrangulaires. L'entrée est composée d'un portique simple aux colonnes doriques, sans aucune décoration sur la porte ou les fenêtres. Le motif du chapiteau dorique, simplifié, se répète sur les piliers des arcades latérales. L'intérieur de la villa a été décoré par Battista Zelotti, qui participa également pour la villa Godi et pour la Malcontenta.

La famiglia di Leonardo Emo possedeva terreni nella località di Fanzolo fin dalla metà del secolo XIV. Quell'area era stata diffusamente romanizzata, come dimostra il tracciato dell'antica via romana e tutto stava ad indicare che la parcellizzazione del territorio seguisse i modelli della stessa epoca. La villa domina tutti i territori che le giacciono attorno all'elevarsi sopra uno zoccolo. La lunga e rettilinea strada di accesso culmina con una rampa che salta il livello del basamento e collega direttamente la facciata principale con il cammino secondo una lunghissima prospettiva che integra il complesso con il paesaggio. Ai fianchi del corpo principale si aggiunsero (per poter conservare i raccolti) due brachese ad arcata semplice che furono poi conclusi con due torri con piccionaie. Questa struttura incornicia la casa nobiliare, che segue lo schema palladiano a pianta quadrata. L'entrata è un semplice portico con colonne doriche, senza alcuna decorazione in porte o finestre. Lo stesso motivo del capitello dorico, semplificato, si ripete anche nei pilastri delle arcate laterali. L'interno della villa fu decorato da Battista Zelotti, che collaborò anche nella villa Godi e nella Malcontenta.

Villa Foscari,
la Malcontenta

Via dei Turisti 9, Malcontenta di Mira, Venice, Italy
1559–1560

The Villa Foscari is a residence without any agricultural outhouses located on the Brenta, the canal that joins Venice to Padua. It is said that this villa's nickname, La Malcontenta, is derived from the sadness experienced by Foscari's wife when she found herself cut off from the city. A portico with six pillars dominates the façade overlooking the canal, as if it were the pronaos of a classical temple. The rear façade, which opens to a small inner garden, imitates the pediment on the front, except that is broken by a large thermal window. This feature is a logical consequence of the internal structure, directly inspired by the Roman baths: the main cross-shape hall is a double-height space that acts as the epicenter of the entire building, effortlessly adapting Roman monumental public architecture to a private house. The whole building seems to be a projection of this central space, from the façades down to the thick base on which it is built. Along with La Rotonda, this is one of Palladio's most admired projects, due to both its structural coherence and the simplicity and coherence of his distinctive use of the classical idiom.

Die Villa Foscari ist eine Residenz ohne landwirtschaftliche Nebengebäude und liegt am Brenta, dem Kanal, der Venedig mit Padua verbindet. Man sagt, dass der Beiname dieser Villa, Malcontenta, von der Traurigkeit der Dame Foscari herrührt, die diese verspürte, wenn sie sich außerhalb der Stadt befand. Ein Portikus mit sechs Säulen beherrscht die zum Kanal hin liegende Fassade, als ob er der Pronaos eines klassischen Tempels wäre. Die hintere Fassade, die sich über einem kleinen Garten erhebt, ahmt den vorderen Portikus nach, allerdings mit dem Unterschied, dass sie von einem großen Thermenfenster durchbrochen wird. Diese Lösung wird von der inneren Struktur vorgegeben, die direkt von den römischen Thermen übernommen wurde. Aus einem kreuzförmigen Grundriss und als Raum mit doppelter Höhe erhebt sich der Hauptsalon wie das Zentrum des gesamten Gebäudes und stellt so die perfekte Anpassung der Monumentalbauweise der römischen öffentlichen Bauten an ein Privathaus dar. Das gesamte Gebäude, von den Fassaden bis hin zum mächtigen Unterbau, über dem sich das Bauwerk erhebt, scheint die Projektion dieses zentralen Raumes zu sein. Gemeinsam mit La Rotonda ist es eines der am meisten bewunderten Projekte Palladios. Dies liegt einerseits an seiner strukturellen Stimmigkeit und andererseits an der ihm eigenen Schlichtheit und Kraft, mit denen Palladio klassische Ausdrucksformen einsetzt.

La villa Foscari est une résidence sans dépendances agricoles, située sur le Brenta, le canal reliant Venise et Padoue. Il est conté que le surnom de cette villa, Malcontenta, vient de la tristesse dont souffrait la dame Foscari en se retirant de la ville. Un portique à six colonnes domine la façade donnant sur le canal, comme s'il s'agissait du pronaos d'un temple classique. La façade postérieure, qui s'élève sur un petit jardin, imite le fronton avant, à la différence qu'il est ouvert par une ample fenêtre thermale. Cette solution naît de sa structure interne, appréhendée directement des thermes romains : situé sur un étage en croix, au cœur d'un espace à double hauteur, le salon principal se dresse en épicentre de tout l'édifice. Il configure ainsi la parfaite adéquation de l'architecture monumentale publique romaine à une maison privée. Toute la demeure semble être la projection de cet espace central, depuis les façades jusqu'au socle épais sur lequel s'érige la maison. Avec la Rotonda, elle constitue un des projets les plus admirés de Palladio, tant pour sa cohérence structurelle que pour sa simplicité et la sûreté de l'emploi particulier qui y est fait du langage classique.

Villa Foscari è una residenza senza dependance situata nel Brenta, il canale che comunica Venezia con Padua. Si dice che il soprannome di questa villa, Malcontenta, derivasse dalla tristezza che le produceva alla dama Foscari il trovarsi isolata dalla città. Un portico con sei colonne domina la facciata che prospetta sul canale, come se si trattasse del pronao di un tempio classico. La facciata posteriore, che si innalza al di sopra di un piccolo giardino, riprende il fronte principale, con la differenza che presenta una grande finestra termale. Questa soluzione deriva dalla struttura interna, desunta direttamente dalle terme romane: ubicato in una pianta cruciforme e in uno spazio a doppia altezza, il salone principale si presenta come il centro dell'intero edificio ed esprime in questo modo il perfetto adeguamento della monumentale architettura romana pubblica ad un edificio privato. Tutto l'edificio sembra essere proiezione di questo spazio centrale, dalle facciate fino al grande basamento sopra a cui si eleva il costruito. Insieme alla Rotonda, la Malcontenta costituisce uno dei progetti più ammirati del Palladio, tanto per la sua coerenza compositiva, quanto per la sua semplicità e rigore con cui viene impiegato il linguaggio classico.

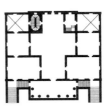

Plan
Grundriss
Niveau
Pianta

Elevation
Aufriss
Élévation
Prospetto

0   5   10

Villa Almerico, la Rotonda

Via della Rotonda 45, Vicenza, Italy
1566–1570

La Rotonda is not strictly speaking a villa, as it has no annexes intended for agricultural purposes and is not set in the middle of the country. In fact, it served as a belvedere, a retreat near the city used for giving parties and relaxing. Palladio himself explained in the "Quattro Libri" that he built a loggia on every side to take advantage of the beautiful views from the hill on which it is set. These vantage points, covered with a pediment, made it impossible to create a main façade, as all the sides follow the same pattern. Even so, there is a strong hierarchical arrangement, with a cupola rising up in the center, visible from all sides, as the culmination of all the façades. It is this feature that provides the sense of roundness from which the name of the building is derived. The emphasis that Palladio placed on the views is crucial to an understanding of why this building was so popular in Anglo-Saxon circles in the centuries to come. The idea of obtaining good views has parallels with present-day thinking, which sees windows not only in practical terms but also as a means to satisfy aesthetic criteria.

La Rotonda ist keine Villa im eigentlichen Sinne, weil sie nicht über Anbauten für landwirtschaftliche Zwecke verfügt und sich auch nicht mitten auf dem Lande befindet. Ihre Funktion ist eigentlich die eines Belvedere, eines Ruheortes in der Nähe der Stadt, an dem man Feste feiern und ausspannen konnte. Palladio selbst erklärt in seinen „Quattro Libri" (Die vier Bücher der Architektur), dass er auf jeder der vier Seiten eine Loggia anbaute, um die schönen Ausblicke auf dem Hügel zu nutzen, auf dem sich das Gebäude erhebt. Diese von einem Giebel bedeckten Erker machen eine Hauptfassade unmöglich, da sämtliche Seiten dasselbe Schema aufweisen. Doch auch so existiert eine starke Hierarchie, da sich in der Mitte des Volumens von allen Seiten sichtbar die Kuppel als Höhepunkt über alle Fassaden erhebt. Es ist dieses Element, das den Eindruck von Rundheit erweckt, die dem Gebäude seinen Namen gibt. Die Bedeutung, die der Architekt den Ausblicken zumisst, ist entscheidend, wenn man verstehen möchte, weshalb dieses Bauwerk in den folgenden Jahrhunderten auf so großen Gefallen in angelsächsischen Breiten stieß. Der Wunsch nach schönen Ausblicken ähnelt der englischen Vorstellung der pittoresken Landschaft und liegt dem heutigen Konzept sehr nahe, nach dem Fenster nicht nur praktischen Zwecken dienen, sondern auch ästhetischen Gesichtspunkten genügen sollen.

La Rotonda n'est pas à proprement parler une villa, car elle ne dispose pas de constructions annexes à des fins agricoles et ne se trouve pas à la campagne. De fait, c'est plutôt un belvédère, un havre de tranquillité près de la ville, pour tenir des fêtes et se reposer. Palladio explique dans les « Quattro Libri » qu'il a construit une loggia pour chaque côté afin de profiter des superbes vues de la colline qui l'accueille. Ces miradors, couverts d'un fronton, rendent impossible toute façade principale, chaque face présentant le même visage architectural. Pour autant, une forte hiérarchie se ressent car s'élève, au centre du volume et visible en tout point, la coupole, point culminant les façades. C'est précisément cet élément qui lui confère la sensation de rondeur. L'importance conférée aux vues par l'architecte est cruciale si l'on souhaite comprendre le motif pour lequel cette œuvre a pu autant captiver le monde anglo-saxon des siècles suivants. L'idée d'obtenir de bonnes vues est parente de la conception anglaise du paysage pittoresque et duc questionnement contemporain, selon lequel les fenêtres n'ont pas uniquement des fins pratiques, mais répondent également à des critères esthétiques.

La Rotonda non è propriamente una villa, dal momento che non dispone di costruzioni annesse con funzioni agricole, né si trova ubicata nel mezzo della campagna. Di fatto, la sua funzione è quella di essere un belvedere, una casa per il riposo vicina alla città in cui celebrare feste e rilassarsi. Lo stesso Palladio nei "Quattro Libri" spiega che aveva costruito una loggia lungo ciascuna facciata per poter sfruttare le belle viste offerte dalla collina su cui si innalzava la costruzione. Questi belvedere, coperti da un frontone, impedivano l'esistenza di una facciata principale, dal momento che tutte i lati presentavano lo stesso schema. Ciò nondimeno esisteva una forte gerarchia d'insieme, elevandosi dal centro del volume una grande cupola, visibile da tutte le parti quale culminazione delle facciate. È questo l'elemento che determina la sensazione di rotondità da cui prende nome l'edificio. L'importanza che l'architetto attribuisce alle viste è cruciale per comprendere la ragione per cui questa opera piacque tanto negli ambienti anglosassoni dei secoli successivi. L'idea di ottenere delle buone viste era affine alla concezione inglese del paesaggio pittoresco ed è molto vicina alle pratiche attuali, secondo cui le finestre non vengono costruite solo con fini pratici, ma anche seguendo dei criteri estetici.

72 Villa Almerico, la Rotonda

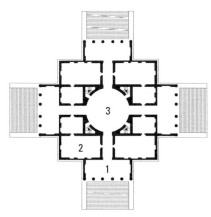

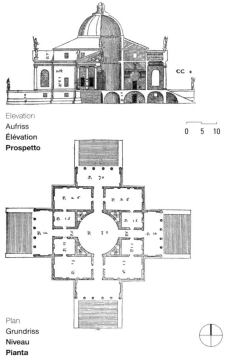

Elevation
Aufriss
Élévation
Prospetto

0 5 10

Plan
Grundriss
Niveau
Pianta

Plan
Grundriss
Niveau
Pianta

1. Access
2. Room
3. Living room

1. Eingang
2. Zimmer
3. Wohnzimmer

1. Accès
2. Chambre
3. Salle de séjour

1. **Entrata**
2. **Stanze**
3. **Salotto**

Villa Almerico, la Rotonda **73**

Chronology of Palladio's works

1508	Born in Padua, christened Andrea di Pietro della Gondola, known as Andrea Palladio.
1537-1542	Villa Godi, Lonedo (designed by Trissino), Italy.
1539-1540	Villa Piovene (central unit without portico), Lonedo, Italy.
1540-1545	Villa Forni-Cerato, Montecchio, Italy.
After 1540	Villa Gazotti-Marcello, Bertesina, Italy.
	Palazzo Civena, Vicenza, Italy.
1541	First visit to Rome with Trissino.
After 1542	Villa Pisani, Bagnolo, Italy.
	Thiene Palace, Vicenza, Italy.
About 1544	Palazzo Porto, Vicenza, Italy.
About 1545	Villa Saraceno, Finale, Italy.
	Villa Thiene, Quinto Vicentino, Italy.
1546-1549	Palladian Basilica, Palazzo della Ragione, Vicenza, Italy.
Before 1550	Villa Poiana, Poiana Maggiore, Italy.
1548-1549	Villa Caldogno, Caldogno, Italy.
1550	Palazzo Chiericati, Vicenza, Italy.
1552	Villa Cornaro, Piombino Dese, Padua, Italy.
1552-1555	Villa Pisani, Montagnana, Trevise, Italy.
1554	Villa Badoer, Fratta Polesine, Rovigo, Italy.
	Villa Barbaro, Maser, Treviso, Italy.
	Palazzo Communal, Feltre, Italy.
About 1555	Villa Chiericati, Vancimuglio di Grumolo delle Abbadesse, Italy.
Before 1556	Facade of the Palazzo Schio, Vicenza, Italy.
1556	Palazzo Antonini, Udine, Italy.
	Bollani Arch, Udine, Italy.

1558	Villa Emo, Fanzolo di Vedelago, Treviso, Italy.
1559-1560	Villa Foscari, la Malcontenta, Malcontenta di Mira, Venice, Italy.
1560-1565	San Giorgio Maggiore, church, refectory and cloister, Venice, Italy.
After 1562	Church of San Francesco della Vigna, façade, Venice, Italy.
1563-1564	Villa Valmarana, Lisiera, Italy.
Before 1565	Palazzo Pretorio, Cividale del Friuli, Italy.
Before 1565	Cathedral, apse and cupola, Vicenza, Italy.
1565-1566	Palazzo Valmarana, Vicenza, Italy.
Before 1566	Villa Zeno, Cessalto, Italy.
1566-1570	Villa Almerico, la Rotonda, Vicenza, Italy.
1568-1569	Villa Serego, Santa Sofia di Pedemonte, Italy.
1570	Palladio publishes "I Quattro Libri dell'Architettura".
1570-1571	Palladio moves to Venice.
	Palazzo Barbarano, Vicenza, Italy.
1571	Capitaniato Loggia, Vicenza, Italy.
Decade of 1570s	Palazzo Porto, Vicenza, Italy.
1576	Valmarana Chapel, Church of Santa Corona, Vicenza, Italy.
1576-1577	Church of Il Redentore, Venice, Italy.
1578	Church of Santa Maria Nuova, Vicenza, Italy.
1579	Porta Gemona, San Daniele del Friuli, Italy.
1579-1580	Olympic Theater, Vicenza, Italy.
1579-1581	Church of Santa Maria della Presentazione, Venice, Italy.
1580	Tempietto in the Villa Barbaro, Maser, Italy.
1580	Palladio dies in Vicenza, on August 19th.

Credits and acknowledgments

Drawings in the specified pages were taken from the following books that belong to the Library of the University of Barcelona:
Barbaro, Daniel: *Vitrvvii Pollionis de architectvra libri decem: cum commentariis Danielis Barbari*, Venice, 1567, in page 9;
Palladio, Andrea: *I Quattri Libri Dell'Architettura di Andrea Palladio*, Venice, 1570, in pages 4, 6, 7, 8 ,16, 20, 22, 46, 53, 56, 68 and 73;
Scamozzi, Bertotti: *Le fabbriche e i disegni di Andrea Palladio*, Genoa, 1843-1846, in pages 11, 29, 30, 34, 37, 40 and 42;
Ortiz Sanz, José Francisco: *Los quatro libros de arquitectura de Andrés Palladio*, Madrid, 1797, in the backcover.

We remain grateful to the antique book department of the University of Barcelona.